Clayton Kershaw

By Jon M. Fishman

AMAZING ATHLETES

Lerner Publications • Minneapolis

Lerner Publications Company
A division of Lerner Publishing Group, Inc.
241 First Avenue North
Minneapolis, MN 55401 USA

For reading levels and more information, look up this title at www.lernerbooks.com.

Library of Congress Cataloging-in-Publication Data

Fishman, Jon M.
    Clayton Kershaw / by Jon M. Fishman.
        pages cm. — (Amazing athletes)
    Includes index.
    ISBN 978-1-4677-5745-4 (lib. bdg. : alk. paper)
    ISBN 978-1-4677-6056-0 (pbk.)
    ISBN 978-1-4677-6213-7 (EB pdf)
    1. Kershaw, Clayton. 2. Baseball players—United States—Biography—Juvenile literature.
3. Pitchers (Baseball)—United States—Biography—Juvenile literature. I. Title.
GV865.K47F57 2015
796.357092—dc23 [B]   2014036038

Manufactured in the United States of America
1 – BP – 12/31/14

TABLE OF CONTENTS

Perfect Pitching   4

Team Player   9

Learning to Pitch   15

"The Whole Package"   19

Big-Hearted Star   23

Selected Career Highlights   29

Glossary   30

Further Reading & Websites   31

Index   32

Clayton Kershaw throws a pitch during a game against the Colorado Rockies on June 18, 2014.

PERFECT PITCHING

Clayton Kershaw held his baseball glove in front of his face. The **ace** pitcher for the Los Angeles Dodgers turned and raised his right leg. Then he sent the ball rocketing toward home plate. Colorado Rockies player Drew Stubbs swung wildly. Strike three!

It was June 18, 2014, in Los Angeles, California. The Dodgers had a huge lead in the eighth inning, 8–0. After striking out Stubbs, Clayton had to get only five more outs to end the game. So far, he hadn't given up a single hit. The young pitcher's first Major League Baseball (MLB) **no-hitter** was in sight.

Clayton has pitched a lot of great games, but he had never thrown an MLB no-hitter.

Clayton winds up for the pitch with two outs in the ninth inning.

Clayton had fired a lot of pitches to make it to the eighth inning. But he wasn't tired yet. Colorado's Josh Rutledge was up next. He swung and missed for strike three. Then Kyle Parker smacked a ground ball, but he was tagged out at first base.

Clayton's teammates join him to celebrate his no-hitter!

In the ninth inning, Clayton got outs with each of his first two pitches. Then he struck out Chris Dickerson to end the game. Clayton's teammates swarmed the pitcher. They hopped up and down and cheered.

The Dodgers used to play in Brooklyn, New York. The team moved to Los Angeles in 1958.

Clayton celebrates his pitching performance against the Colorado Rockies.

Clayton had thrown a no-hitter!

The *Los Angeles Times* called the no-hitter "MLB's all-time best" pitching performance. Clayton had struck out 15 Rockies batters in the game. He hadn't issued a single **walk**. "This is pretty special," Clayton said. "I will remember this forever."

Clayton started playing baseball at a young age.

TEAM PLAYER

Clayton Edward Kershaw was born on March 19, 1988, in Dallas, Texas. He lived in nearby Highland Park. Clayton's mother's name is Marianne. His father, Chris, passed away in 2013.

As a child, Clayton played team sports such as baseball and soccer. He became close friends with one of his teammates, Matthew Stafford. Matthew often played **catcher** when Clayton pitched Little League games. "We always worked well together playing baseball," Clayton

said. Matthew's best sport was football. Years later, he became the quarterback of the Detroit Lions in the National Football League (NFL).

Matthew Stafford throws a pass during an NFL game in 2009.

Chris and Marianne divorced when their son was 10 years old. Clayton lived with his mother, a graphic designer. Most of the people who lived in Highland Park had plenty of money. But Marianne and her son weren't as wealthy as their neighbors. "We didn't have a lot of money," Clayton said. "I don't know how she did it."

Highland Park is a scenic town in northeast Texas.

Clayton attended Highland Park High School. It had one of the most successful **sports programs** in Texas. Highland Park had won

state titles in tennis and swimming and many other sports. But football was the top sport at the school.

Clayton rests on the bench during a high school football game.

In 2003, Clayton played **center** on Highland Park's freshman football team. His friend Matthew was the quarterback. Matthew and Clayton also

Chris Young, a pitcher for the Seattle Mariners, also attended Highland Park High School. He graduated in 1998.

played together on the baseball team. But the athletes blossomed in different sports. After freshman year, Clayton quit the football team. Matthew stopped playing baseball after his sophomore season.

By his senior season, Clayton was the best player on the Highland Park baseball team.

LEARNING TO PITCH

Clayton worked hard to become a better pitcher after he stopped playing football. He began lifting weights. By his senior year, Clayton's body was full of muscle. He also grew to six feet three inches tall.

Outside of team practice, he trained with Skip Johnson. Johnson was a baseball coach at nearby Navarro College at the time. He and Clayton practiced pitching together once a week for almost three months. "That was actually the first real pitching lesson I ever had," Clayton said.

Working with Coach Johnson paid off. Clayton's pitches were faster than ever. In a game against Northwest High School in May 2006, he struck out all 15 batters he faced. Clayton also hit a home run to help his team win the game.

Skip Johnson helped Clayton become a highly skilled pitcher.

As a senior, Clayton had a perfect record of 13 wins and zero losses for Highland Park. He struck out 139 batters in 64 innings. His **earned run average (ERA)** was an incredible 0.77. *Baseball America* wrote a story about Clayton. They called him "the top high school **prospect**" in the country.

Clayton drew the attention of **scouts** from all around the country. Many colleges offered him **scholarships**. In June 2006, MLB held its annual **draft**.

Five pitchers were chosen before Clayton in the 2006 MLB draft. None of them have been as successful as Clayton.

Clayton *(top row, second from right)* poses with the 2006 Highland Park High School baseball team.

The Los Angeles Dodgers chose Clayton with the seventh overall pick.

The young pitcher had a tough decision to make. He could take one of the scholarships and go to college. Or he could start playing professional baseball right away. Clayton's first college choice was Texas A&M University. His girlfriend, Ellen, was set to attend the school that fall. But Clayton couldn't pass up the chance to get paid to play baseball. He decided not to go to college.

In 2006, Clayton pitched for Team USA at the game against the World Futures Team at AT&T Park in San Francisco,

"THE WHOLE PACKAGE"

The Dodgers wanted Clayton to gain experience in the **minor leagues**. They would call him up to play with the major-league team when they thought he was ready. In

2006, Clayton pitched in 10 games for the Gulf Coast League Dodgers. The team played in Vero Beach, Florida. Clayton gave up just 10 total runs in those games for an ERA of 1.95.

Clayton began the next season with the Great Lakes Loons, a minor-league team in Midland, Michigan. Then he moved on to the Jacksonville Suns of Jacksonville, Florida. His combined ERA for the two teams was 2.95. He struck out 163 batters in 122 innings.

Clayton pitches for the Loons in 2011.

In 2008, the Dodgers assigned Clayton to Jacksonville again. But he didn't stay with the team for long. After pitching in 13 games for the Suns, the Dodgers called Clayton to the major leagues.

Clayton's first MLB game was in Los Angeles against the St. Louis Cardinals. He allowed two runs in six innings. Clayton struck out seven batters and gave up only five hits. The Dodgers won the game, 4–3.

Dodgers pitching coach Rick Honeycutt was impressed with Clayton.

The Dodgers have won the World Series five times. Only three teams have won it more often.

"He's just a great kid, willing to learn," Honeycutt said. "He's the whole package." Clayton pitched in 22 games for the Dodgers in 2008. But his 4.26 ERA for the season showed that he still had some learning to do.

In 2009, he pitched for Los Angeles all season. His 2.79 ERA was eighth best in MLB. He struck out 185 batters in 171 innings. The next season, Clayton had the league's 12th-best ERA at 2.91. After just two MLB seasons, Clayton had become one of the game's best pitchers.

Clayton pitches for the Dodgers during a game against the Arizona Diamondbacks.

Clayton poses with his wife, Ellen, at an event in 2012.

BIG-HEARTED STAR

In December 2010, Clayton and longtime-girlfriend Ellen got married. The two began planning a trip to Zambia in Africa. Ellen had already been to Zambia four times. Many people in the country are poor and hungry.

In 2012, Clayton won the Roberto Clemente Award. Each year, MLB gives the award to a player who helps others outside of baseball. Clayton became the youngest player to ever earn the award.

Ellen wanted to help.

One month after their wedding, Ellen and Clayton traveled to Zambia. They learned about the country. They spent time with children such as Hope, a young girl whose parents had died. The experience had a big effect on Clayton. "It changes you, and that's a good thing," he said. Clayton left Zambia determined to help the children he met.

The 2011 season was Clayton's finest yet. He won 21 games and lost only five. His 2.28 ERA led all major-league pitchers. Clayton earned the 2011 Cy Young Award as the best pitcher in

MLB's National League (NL). "It's just so special and I'm not taking it for granted," Clayton said. "I'm just soaking it all in right now."

Clayton has also volunteered with Habitat for Humanity. The group helps build and repair homes for people in need around the world.

In 2012, Clayton's ERA of 2.53 was tops in MLB for the second year in a row.

Clayton and Ellen traveled to Lusaka, Zambia, after the 2012 season. Using their own money, the Kershaws built a home for children without parents. They named it Hope's Home

Clayton pitches against the St. Louis Cardinals at Dodger Stadium.

after the girl they'd met in 2011. "Now, for the first time, these kids have a bed to call their own," Ellen said. "For the first time, these kids have three meals a day."

In 2013, Clayton posted an incredible 1.83 ERA over 236 innings. He was awarded the

Cy Young for the second time. The Dodgers finished the season in first place in their **division** by a whopping 11 games. But Los Angeles lost to the Cardinals in the **playoffs**.

In October 2014, the Dodgers finished in first place in the NL West. Clayton reached the top of his game, leading MLB in ERA and wins. "He's the best pitcher on the planet right now," Dodgers catcher A. J. Ellis said. "There's nobody even close."

The Dodgers celebrate a win.

Clayton signs autographs for
excited fans before a game.

Clayton loves baseball. But he's proud of
the work he and Ellen are doing in Africa too.
"Obviously I'm passionate about baseball, and
I love it," Clayton said. "But off-the-field stuff
[such as Hope's Home] means more." Clayton's
passion has made him a star on and off the
baseball field.

Selected Career Highlights

2014 Named to the MLB All-Star Game for the fourth time
Finished the season with the best ERA in MLB (1.77),

2013 Finished the season with the best ERA in MLB (1.83)
Named to the MLB All-Star Game for the third time
Opened Hope's Home in Zambia, Africa, with wife, Ellen
Won Cy Young Award for the second time

2012 Became the youngest person to win the Roberto Clemente Award
Finished the season with the best ERA in MLB (2.53)
Named to the MLB All-Star Game for the second time

2011 Finished the season with the best ERA in MLB (2.28)
Named to the MLB All-Star Game for the first time
Won Cy Young Award for the first time

2010 Finished the season with the 12th-best ERA in MLB (2.91)

2009 Finished the season with the 8th-best ERA in MLB (2.79)

2008 Pitched in 22 games for the Los Angeles Dodgers
Pitched in 13 games for the Jacksonville Suns

2007 Pitched in five games for the Jacksonville Suns
Pitched in 20 games for the Great Lakes Loons

2006 Pitched in 10 games for the Gulf Coast League Dodgers
Chosen by the Los Angeles Dodgers in the MLB draft
Had a perfect record of 13–0 as a senior at Highland Park High School

Glossary

ace: the top pitcher on a baseball team

catcher: the player behind home plate who catches throws from the pitcher

center: the player on a football team who hands the ball to the quarterback at the beginning of each play

division: a group of teams that play against one another. The MLB has six divisions.

draft: a yearly event in which professional teams take turns choosing new players from a selected group

earned run average (ERA): the average number of runs allowed by a pitcher every nine innings

minor leagues: groups of teams where players improve their skills and prepare to advance to MLB

no-hitter: a game in which a pitcher throws a complete game and doesn't give up a hit

playoffs: a series of games played at the end of the season to determine a champion

prospect: a young baseball player that scouts think is likely to get better as the player gets older

scholarships: money given to students by schools or other groups to help pay for school

scouts: people who judge the abilities of athletes

sports programs: the sets of sports available for students to play at schools

walk: when the batter is allowed to take first base after the pitcher throws four balls outside of the strike zone

Further Reading & Websites

Doeden, Matt. *The World Series: Baseball's Biggest Stage*. Minneapolis: Millbrook Press, 2014.

Kennedy, Mike, and Mark Stewart. *Long Ball: The Legend and Lore of the Home Run*. Minneapolis: Millbrook Press, 2006.

Major League Baseball: The Official Site
http://mlb.mlb.com/home
The official Major League Baseball website provides fans with game results, statistics, schedules, and biographies of players.

The Official Site of the Los Angeles Dodgers
http://losangeles.dodgers.mlb.com/index.jsp?c_id=la
The official website of the Los Angeles Dodgers includes the team schedule and game results, biographies of Clayton Kershaw and other players and coaches, and much more.

Sports Illustrated Kids
http://www.sikids.com
The *Sports Illustrated Kids* website covers all sports, including baseball.

LERNER

SOURCE

Expand learning beyond the printed book. Download free, complementary educational resources for this book from our website, www.lerneresource.com.

Index

Baseball America, 16

Ellis, A. J., 27

Great Lakes Loons, 20
Gulf Coast League Dodgers, 20

Honeycutt, Rick, 21
Hope's Home, 25–26, 28

Jacksonville Suns, 20, 21
Johnson, Skip, 15–16

Kershaw, Chris (father), 9, 11
Kershaw, Clayton: awards, 24, 26–27; charity work, 25–26, 28; childhood, 10–11; high school years, 12–13, 15–16; minor-league career, 19–21; MLB games, 4–8, 21–22; training, 15–16
Kershaw, Ellen (wife), 18, 23–26, 28
Kershaw, Marianne (mother), 9, 11

Los Angeles Dodgers, 4–5, 7, 18–19, 21–22, 27

Major League Baseball (MLB) draft (2006), 17–18

Stafford, Matthew, 10, 13

Photo Acknowledgmen[ts]

The images in this book are use[d]
Decolongon/Getty Images, pp. 4,
pp. 9, 12, 14, 17; © Tom Cammett
© Twilight Photography/Alamy, [
© Rich Pilling/MLB Photos via Ge
Four Seam Images, p. 20; © Lisa [
Merritt/Getty Images, p. 23; © Ma
© Jeff Gross/Getty Images, p. 26;
Cunningham/Getty Images, p. 28

Front cover: © Victor Decolongon

Main body text set in Caecilia LT
Typeface provided by Adobe Syst[ems]